THE GHOSTLY TALES OF PUGET SOUND

Published by Arcadia Children's Books
A Division of Arcadia Publishing, Inc.
Charleston, SC
www.arcadiapublishing.com

Copyright © 2025 by Arcadia Children's Books
All rights reserved

Spooky America is a trademark of Arcadia Publishing, Inc.

First published 2025
Manufactured in the United States

Designed by Jessica Nevins
Images used courtesy of Shutterstock.com; p. 30 Underawesternsky/Shutterstock.com;
p. 38 BLAZE Pro/Shutterstock.com; p. 60 Brian Logan Photography/Shutterstock.com;
p. 74 vewfinder/Shutterstock.com; p. 96 Ian Dewar Photography/Shutterstock.com.

ISBN: 9781467197908
Library of Congress Control Number: 2024950519

Notice: The information in this book is true and complete to the best of our
knowledge. It is offered without guarantee on the part of the author or Arcadia
Publishing. The author and Arcadia Publishing disclaim all liability in connection with
the use of this book.

All rights reserved. No part of this book may be reproduced or transmitted in any form
whatsoever without prior written permission from the publisher except in the case of
brief quotations embodied in critical articles and reviews.

Spooky America

THE GHOSTLY TALES OF PUGET SOUND

STACIA DEUTSCH

Adapted from Haunted Puget Sound by Ira Wesley Kitmacher

Washington

Puget Sound

Canada

Pacific Ocean

Oregon

Table of Contents & Map Key

Welcome to Spooky Puget Sound!.............3
Chapter 1. A Haunted History of Puget Sound.............9
1 Chapter 2. Odd Things in Olympia.............15
Chapter 3. Spooky Sites Outside Olympia.............31
- **2** Bordeaux
- **3** Bucoda
- **4** Centralia
- **5** Joint Base Lewis-McChord
- **6** McNeil Island
- **7** Steilacoom

8 Chapter 4. Terrifying Tales from Tacoma.............39
Chapter 5. Terrible Travels Outside Tacoma.............53
- **9** Algona
- **10** Carbonado
- **11** Graham
- **12** Olalla
- **13** Lakewood
- **14** Puyallup

15 Chapter 6. Super-scares in Seattle.............61
Chapter 7. More Ghosts Gather Near Seattle.............75
- **16** Bainbridge Island
- **17** Bremerton
- **18** Des Moines
- **19** Edmonds
- **20** Kent
- **21** Port Orchard

22 Chapter 8. Eerie Everett.............85
Chapter 9. Small Towns with Spooky Spirits.............89
- **23** Port Gamble
- **24** Whidbey Island
- **25** Friday Harbor

26 Chapter 10. Who's Haunting Bellingham?.............97
Chapter 11. The Final Frights.............101
- **27** Port Townsend
- **28** Port Angeles
- **29** Lake Crescent

A Ghostly Goodbye.............107

Welcome to Spooky Puget Sound!

People look for ghosts for many reasons. For those who believe in the supernatural, stories about hauntings provide proof. Sometimes ghost stories explain mysterious things. And, for some, ghost stories are simply fun.

In the area of Puget Sound, along the northwest coast of Washington State, these stories combine legends with history. They give us a peek into some of the things that make the region special.

While bays connect to one body of water, a *sound* connects to multiple. Puget Sound is the system of interconnected waterways and basins that flow around the northwest coast of Washington State. Along the sound, you'll find the haunted cities of Tacoma, Seattle, Everett, Bellingham, and many other towns.

The region was named "Puget Sound" by British explorer George Vancouver. Vancouver was best known for his 1791–1795 expedition charting North America's northwestern Pacific coast regions. He sailed his ship, the HMS *Discovery* to areas later known as Alaska, British Columbia, Oregon, and Washington. Puget Sound was named in honor of his second lieutenant, Peter Puget, who explored the main channel of the sound. Before it was called Puget Sound, the Coastal Salish Indigenous peoples, who had lived in the region for thousands of years, called the area "Whulge," meaning "sea, salt water, ocean, or sound."

About one hundred miles in length, Puget Sound is the second-largest estuary in the United States. Chesapeake Bay, along the East Coast, is the largest. (An estuary occurs where a mixture of fresh water draining from the land meets salty seawater.) If you are visiting, look out for bald eagles, black bears, elk, and deer. The best way to see those is by getting out in nature: hiking, boating, camping, fishing, or biking. You can visit state parks that have nineteenth-century military forts and national historic sites.

But beware!

While Washington State offers breathtaking scenery, the cities along the shores of Puget Sound are also known as some of the spookiest places in America. The spirits of frontiersmen, adventurers, boatmen, and early settlers have been spotted in almost every town. There are older spirits, like those of the Indigenous peoples who were here first. And as we hunt for haunts, you'll see the area has also had its share of sailors, soldiers, and unfortunately, murders and murder victims.

There are so many chilling tales from Puget Sound that you shouldn't be surprised by all the books and movie ideas that come from the area. The vampire and werewolf *Twilight* books (and movies) were set here. The pirate treasure movie *The Goonies*, the TV series *Supernatural*, the remake of *The Fog*, and the drama-mystery *Twin Peaks* were all made or based in or near Puget Sound.

Are you curious to find out more?

Come visit Puget Sound's possessed parks and creepy underground tunnels. There are hotels with ghostly guests. Some areas, including Seattle, have many haunted houses—not just at Halloween, but all the time!

Some ghosts like the country. Others, the city. There are new haunts and ancient places. The local weather is also a mirror for the spirits and their moods. The dark skies, wind, and fog make the area feel mysterious and frightening.

While it's easy to proclaim, *Ghosts don't exist*, a lot of people have had believable experiences. It's time to ask yourself...

Do YOU believe in ghosts?

Turn the page and decide for yourself.

A Haunted History of Puget Sound

Puget Sound is a scenic area made up of deep waters, tall mountains, thick rainforests, and lots of wildlife.

If you measured the coastline around Puget Sound, it would be about 1,332 miles long. That means it would take about eighteen days to walk the entire shore, but it's impossible because there's no direct route and some of the land is off limits to visitors.

The area's history goes back at least ten thousand years. Puget Sound's Indigenous population migrated from Asia. They walked across a land bridge that connected Asia and North America, seeking a place that had all the resources they needed: wood, fish, oysters and other shellfish, deer and other mammals, herbs, and birds.

In 1774, just before the American Revolution, Spanish explorers came to the area. Then, the British arrived. The area wasn't under the control of the United States until June 15, 1846, when the official border separating the United States from Canada was established.

The border caused a lot of problems. Many people went to sleep in one country and woke up in another. Laws differed depending on if you were in the United States or Canada. Indigenous tribes were forced to move. It was a time of chaos, but eventually, people settled down and the Pacific Northwest was quiet for a while.

In 1854, Chief Leschi of the Nisqually tribe negotiated the Treaty of Medicine Creek. This treaty protected some Indigenous areas, but in 1855, gold was discovered in eastern Washington. Eager miners began searching for gold on tribal lands.

After several miners were killed, the territorial governor forced the Indigenous peoples to move to reservations. Wars took place between the United States and Indigenous peoples, including the Puget Sound War of 1855–1856. Many people on both sides died in the fighting.

In the end, U.S. troops caught and hanged Chief Leschi. And yet . . . some say his spirit never

left. In fact, ever since that day in 1858, his ghost has been repeatedly seen around Steilacoom, where he died.

In 1862, many Americans from the Eastern United States moved to the region as a result of the government's Homestead Act. Under the Homestead Act, a person could claim 160 acres of government land, as long as they lived on and "improved" their plot. Thousands of people headed west, and the government officially gave them land that had been home to the Indigenous tribes in the area.

The tribes lost their homes while cities quickly grew on their lands. The cities became bigger and bigger, making Puget Sound an important part of Washington State's economy, culture, and environment. Now, nearly two-thirds of the state's population live in this area. There are busy ports for big ships that carry products and passengers every day. The military even has a naval shipyard at Bremerton.

Look around and you'll see more than cities. Puget Sound's marine life is amazing, too: dolphins, giant Pacific octopuses, gray whales, humpback whales, orcas, porpoises, sea lions, and sea otters, as well as clams, mussels, anemones, sea stars, and crabs. If you're lucky, you might spot a six-gill shark, which can be sixteen to twenty feet long!

There's a lot of history surrounding Puget Sound, and hundreds of thousands of people moved to the area over time. So, of course that means there are a lot of ghost stories told by Indigenous peoples, explorers, and settlers. Haunted tales have been passed down for centuries. Let's start listening to the spirits. We'll begin at the southernmost point on Puget Sound, Olympia, and from there, move north and westward.

The ghosts are eager to tell you all about their home in Puget Sound.

Governor's Mansion

Odd Things in Olympia

Olympia is the capital of Washington. Sixty miles southwest of Seattle, the state's biggest city, people love Olympia because it's a "cool" cultural center. It's no surprise that ghosts like hanging out here, too!

Back in 1846, Olympia was called Smithfield. Edmund Sylvester and Levi Lathrop Smith claimed the land that is now downtown Olympia. Two years later, Smith was on his way to an

Oregon Territorial Legislature meeting when he had a seizure. He fell out of a rowboat and drowned.

In 1850, the town officially became "Olympia," thanks to the amazing views of the Olympic Mountains to the northwest. In November 1851, a large sailing ship called *Exact* took passengers to Alki Point, which is the point of land where the city of Seattle began. When the winter storms calmed, A. Denny, C.D. Boren, and William N. Bell, sailed south toward Olympia. There, they discovered that the water was deep enough to establish a port. The three men staked land claims and began to build. A short time after that, Olympia became the capital of the new Washington Territory. (The Washington Territory broke off from Oregon Territory in 1853, and Washington became a state in 1889.)

When settlers from the east moved west, many came in wagons. The Oregon Trail started in Missouri and wound two thousand miles across the Rocky Mountains into Oregon's Willamette Valley. The northernmost spur of the trail ended in Olympia's Sylvester Park. It's estimated that 300,000 to 400,000 immigrants used the Oregon Trail between 1840 and 1860.

The trail was dangerous. About thirty thousand people died on the trip. Most of the deaths were from diseases, but people also fell off their wagons and were run over. Some were killed by gun mishaps, drowning, weather, or fights. Ghosts from the Oregon Trail are known to haunt Sylvester Park. Here, pioneers are seen wandering around, as if they never settled down. And, it's not just the ghosts of the pioneers hanging around the park, but also ghosts from the Puget Sound War of 1855–1856. And for those who suffered trauma and died along the Oregon Trail, the park is the perfect place to haunt.

Unlike the Oregon Trail ghosts that wander

around Olympia, some ghosts are stuck in the place where their trauma occurred. The Avanti High School of Olympia is a place like that. The school used to be called the Old Washington School. It dates back to 1924. The first reported ghostly sighting was in the 1950s. It's said that a worker fell while painting a railing near a fourth-floor window. After his death, witnesses claimed his ghost slammed windows and doors, locking them out. Spooked students heard sounds echoing in the hallways, disembodied footsteps, and sometimes, they'd see movement in shadowy corners.

And for some ghosts, it's impossible to know the reasons behind their chosen haunts. Who are these ghosts, and why are they in certain places? If only the ghosts could tell us their stories. Instead, they linger in shadows and spooky dark corners, keeping their secrets to themselves.

The oldest house in Olympia, the gothic Bigelow House, was built during the 1850s.

Today, it is a museum. Occasionally, in the evening when the sun is just setting, employees report seeing the phantom of a distinguished gentleman. He'd linger, looking at the displays, but disappear when someone approached. It's thought this might be the ghost of Daniel Bigelow, a lawyer and politician who lived in the house. Is it possible that he never left after he died in 1905?

If you are interested in visiting more spirits of the past, visit The Brotherhood Lounge on Capitol Way in Olympia, built in 1890. This was a place for loggers, longshoremen, railroad workers, and workers to hang out. Some of the union members never quit visiting the lodge—even after they died. There's a sign outside that reads "Labor Temple," and since the members were a brotherhood, the place is often called "Broho." The façade used to be ornate and beautiful, but in 1949, it was heavily damaged in an earthquake. There are photos that show the living who visited this place, like President John F. Kennedy and actor Bruce Lee. Now, the celebrities are gone, but friendly spirits remain.

One employee reported seeing shadows of people cast against a wall at night. The employee was alone.

Another employee claims she's heard her name whispered in her ear. She was alone.

The spirits never do harm but seem to be enjoying the place, just like they remember, all those years ago.

Next, visit the Olympia's Capitol House Apartments on Sherman Street, which used to be St. Peter's Hospital. The hospital operated there from the 1880s to 1923, when it was renamed the Sherman Street Hospital. The hospital closed in the 1960s.

People living in the current apartments have reported many ghosts there. One longtime resident said they'd seen an elderly lady rocking back and forth in a rocking chair in the lobby.

The resident moved forward to investigate, but as she did, her friend called her name—when she turned back, the ghost was gone.

Another apartment resident remarked, "It's an old hospital; people died here all the time. I'm sure it's haunted. I've seen a ghost."

And if those stories aren't scary enough, check out the Capitol Theater, built in 1924. The theater once served as an Odd Fellows Lodge. At times, it was also a movie palace and theater. In 1937, a fire burned most of the original features in the interior, but the building was renovated. Furniture and carpets can be tossed out, but the ghosts stay behind no matter what. It's even said that a murder happened in the theater in the 1930s or '40s.

There were so many stories of ghosts in the theater that the Paranormal Investigations of Historic America (PIHA) set up its equipment and investigated the theater in 2010. Their video evidence is on YouTube. The investigators found ghostly orbs. They used electronic voice phenomena (EVP) and electromagnetic field (EMF) devices to detect voices and movement and found both. There were spirits in the theater's green room, dressing room, and mezzanine.

The group officially labeled the place "haunted."

The best-known ghost at the theater is an elderly movie lover. He might have died in the theater, or maybe he just loved being there so much that he never wanted to leave. It seems he also loves his privacy. If anyone approaches him, he disappears.

Up next, check out the Georgia Pacific manufacturing building, where the ghost of another elderly man wanders. Since the 1950s, employees have reported this hunched, slow-moving, shadowy figure lingering after closing. There might be other ghosts, too. Some

have seen a blob-shaped entity floating up to the ceiling. Another employee reported that while talking to themselves in the customer service area, a disembodied voice answered them.

Two young ghosts hang out at the governor's mansion. This old building sits on twelve acres in Olympia with legislative buildings and parks. In 1908, the mansion was erected as a temporary structure. Earthquakes in 1949 and 2001 damaged the building, but Washington governors and their families continue to live there.

In 1997, a creepy thing happened to Governor Gary Locke and his family while they occupied the mansion. They were forced to leave after bats moved in. They all had to get rabies vaccinations, just in case!

Pest control removed the bats, but the spirit of a small boy wearing a blue sailor suit riding an antique tricycle remained. In the 1960s, a tour group reportedly saw the child on his tricycle.

Some waved at him. Later, the group heard the sound of a ball bouncing. Was it the same child? Members of the group asked the guide, "Who was that boy?" The guide confessed that the mansion was haunted by the spirits of *two* little boys. But in the 1970s, sightings of the ghost on the tricycle stopped, so people believe it has moved on. However, the sounds of the phantom bouncing ball remain. None of the past governor's children died in the house, so no one knows who these ghost children might be.

In nearby Lacey, on June 27, 1934, a dynamite factory called J. A. Denn exploded. Eleven people died: ten male employees and a thirty-seven-year-old woman named Hazel Epley. Today, some people claim that Hazel Epley's poltergeist still haunts the neighboring area. (A poltergeist is a mischievous ghost supposedly responsible for strange noises and objects being thrown around.) She is not friendly—often hitting and scratching residents near the factory site. There are a few reports of the others who died, but those ghosts aren't angry. Rather, they seem confused about what may have happened.

Olympia's Old State Capitol Building was built in 1892 as the Thurston County Courthouse and served as the state's first capitol from 1905 to 1928. Now, it serves as a home for government offices. Everyone calls the building "the Castle" because it looks like one. It's four stories high and has nineteen rooms. Once upon a time, the building had a 150-foot-tall central clock tower with an illuminated clock face on each of its eight sides. It was so bright that Olympia residents could see it from a distance. The tower was destroyed in a fire in 1928. Then, the original turrets toppled in the 1949 earthquake. Now fully renovated, the capitol is known as one of the most haunted historic buildings in town.

The Olympia Police are frequently called to the building at night because the security system has been set off, but they never find anyone trying to break in.

Two police officers claim to have experienced something ghostly in the building, one of them saying that he was nervous and got the "willies" there at night. The other officer commented, "Ask any of the night staff [about the hauntings]; they'll tell you."

Nearby is the Spar Café, which is part of McMenamin's hotel and restaurant chain. The chain often makes "most haunted" lists. Employees and visitors report "being watched" by nonhuman entities. Sometimes, they feel someone or something that is not physically present. Objects are also known to move around.

The Spar Café sits over a tunnel rumored to have been used during Prohibition. (In the United States, Prohibition was put in place by the Eighteenth Amendment, and from1920 to

1933, the manufacture, sale, and transportation of alcohol was against the law). One employee said the basement, where the tunnel is located, is "creepy," and "where the ghosts are."

Just like the Capitol Theater, the State Theater, built in 1949, is also said to be haunted. In fact, many theaters have ghost lamps to keep away mischievous ghosts when the theater is empty. Some people think that theaters are natural homes for ghosts because the actors and politicians who stood on stage often had strong opinions and feelings. Big emotions bring out spirits.

Even when alone, visitors have reported strange movements, disembodied noises, and cold spots. This building was also used at one time as a jail, so maybe the ghostly entities seen in the State Theater are those of prisoners awaiting trial.

Finally, the most haunted place in all of Olympia is possibly the Forest Memorial Gardens

Cemetery, established in April 1857. Here, ghosts have been seen wandering around the tombstones. There are reports of disembodied footsteps and voices. Cold spots and temperature changes also indicate ghosts are present. Some spirits may belong to Olympia's pioneer families, who are buried there, but this was also where unknown and unclaimed bodies were buried. If you're looking for ghosts, it's always smart to check out the local cemetery. Forest Memorial Gardens Cemetery is a good place to start!

About three thousand miles east of Olympia, in Philadelphia, Pennsylvania, there is a ship named after the city of Olympia, the USS *Olympia*. The ship was built in San Francisco and went into service in 1895. It's the United States' oldest preserved steel warship, having served in the Spanish-American War in 1898. The *Olympia* saw action in World War I and was in service until 1922.

While many old ships are haunted, the USS *Olympia* is said to be one of the most haunted vessels. During its long service, nineteen men died onboard. Some visitors who have taken the ghost tour have reported feeling someone grab them in the engine room. Phantom faces appear in mirrors, shadowy ghosts roam the halls, and—in quiet moments—disembodied voices can be heard echoing down empty corridors.

Olympia is the capital of Washington, but it may also be the spookiest city in Washington State.

Centralia, Washington

Spooky Sites Outside Olympia

Bordeaux is fifteen minutes south of Olympia. Built in the early 1900s, the town sat at the edge of a busy lumber yard. By 1941, the town had a school, a post office, a lumber mill, and a railroad that led to and from the nearby forests. Later, when the lumber industry took a downward turn, the mill closed, and the townspeople moved on.

It's now a ghost town. Only a few brick, wood,

and concrete structures remain. And yet, visitors to the abandoned area have described meeting full-body apparitions of lumberjacks walking from their old workstations toward what used to be the bank vault. Perhaps they're hoping to still get paid?

Another small town called Bucoda is twenty miles south of Olympia. Only 562 people live there, but so do a lot of ghosts. The town's original name was Seatco, a Native American word meaning "evil spirit" or "devil." There are so many spirits in town that every October the place is called "Boo-coda" and hosts events like casket races, hearse processions, a zombie 5K race, jack-o'-lantern carving contests, and a haunted house.

But in addition to those fun events, keen eyes might spot a ghostly figure wearing striped prisoner's clothing. The town was the site of Washington's first territorial prison from 1874 to 1888. The place was rumored to be so brutal to the prisoners that the facility's nickname was "Hell on Earth."

In 2009, Bucoda contracted a painter to work on the Halloween haunted house. The attraction took place inside an old gym, originally built in the 1930s. Late one night, the artist was painting the image of a little girl on the wall. He turned around when he heard giggling. Nobody was there. But then, as he got back to work, he heard a voice whisper, "Boo!"

The painter quit for the night, telling town officials that he would never work alone in that building again. He was right to be worried. Two years later, paranormal investigators investigated the Bucoda Gym and found many ghostly orbs.

It's rumored that in Centralia, twenty-two miles south of Olympia, the historic Olympic Club Hotel and Saloon was the scene of several murders. Employees reported seeing ghostly orbs, shadows of people who weren't there, and mist or ectoplasm throughout the hotel. Plus, they heard disembodied voices, footsteps, and the sounds of other movements emanating from vacant rooms.

Joint Base Lewis-McChord, a military base shared by the U.S. Army, Air Force, Marines, and Navy, is located between Olympia and Tacoma. It's not only the soldiers and pilots who are busy there—ghosts are haunting the base. Those who live and work there have reported hearing the cries of Indigenous peoples who were forced to leave their land. Disembodied chanting and singing echo late at night. Ghostly soldiers march across the compound.

Among the ghosts is a man who was killed in 1927, during the filming of the World War I–based silent movie *The Patent Leather Kid*. His spirit is frequently seen in the area, accompanied by his own disembodied sounds, crying, cold spots, and alarms that go off at random. Is he angry or sad? It's unclear, but building management summoned three priests to the building to perform an exorcism. (An exorcism is a religious practice used to get rid of evil spirits from a place or person.) One of the priests said that a cowboy appeared before them. The cowboy claimed that he had caused his own death. The priests told him that he was "forgiven" and that it was "okay to leave." The cowboy's ghost finally faded away.

McNeil Island (nicknamed the Alcatraz of the Pacific Northwest) is an island in Puget Sound between Olympia and Tacoma. For generations, the island was a fishing location for Coastal Salish Indigenous peoples. But for over a hundred years, from 1875 to 1976, McNeil Island served as a federal penitentiary. By 1947, the population was 320 inmates. Some famous prisoners, including Robert "Birdman of Alcatraz" Stroud and Charles Manson, lived in those cells.

From 1981 to 2011, the island was converted to a state correctional facility. Currently, it's a state special commitment center, confining over one hundred dangerous people. Prisons are known to have ghosts, and this one has *many*.

The town of Steilacoom was one of the earliest non-tribal settlements in the area. The Captain Edwin R. Rogers House was built in Steilacoom in 1891. Rogers was a wealthy sea merchant. His wife, Catherine, and their large family lived there until Rogers lost most of their money in 1893. Two years later, the mansion became the Waverly Hotel. It was also a museum and a restaurant before it became law offices in 2006.

Chief Leschi (remember him from Chapter 1?) was hanged in 1858 on gallows near the house. Many have seen his spirit looking out at Puget Sound. Or perhaps the spirit is a guest from the hotel days who was mugged and killed? *Or*, maybe it's Edwin R. Rogers, who built the place? Are you brave enough to ask the ghost who he is?

A ghostly woman is also hanging around the mansion. She's seen wearing a white dress and floating near the ceiling in the restaurant. Over the years, guests have heard footsteps and seen a disembodied woman's legs. But what about the rest of her? Could this be the same elegantly dressed woman with an old-fashioned hairstyle who guests have seen reflected in mirrors and windows? We may never know for certain. What we *can* be sure of is that this mansion has no shortage of spooky activity!

A man who died in a fight on the grounds has been seen going up an invisible staircase. Unexplained electrical surges happen, and there are strange footprints in the carpet. Occasionally, candles and glasses have been thrown off tables by unseen hands.

If you think you'll be getting away from ghosts by getting out of Olympia—think again. There are *plenty* of scary things lurking in the surrounding towns and cities. So grab your flashlight and turn the page... if you dare!

Terrifying Tales from Tacoma

Tacoma is the second-largest city (by population) in the Puget Sound region. The town is called "Pretty Grit City" because it started out as a rough and tumble town—and has beautiful views.

The Puyallup people lived in settlements throughout the area long before settlers came. Swedish settler, Nicholas De Lin, arrived in 1852. He was responsible for the region's first sawmill.

As the city grew, it was named Tacoma City, which is the Indigenous name for a mountain nearby.

Tacoma was incorporated in 1875, after it was selected to be the westernmost stop of the Northern Pacific Railroad. The railroad brought workers and businesses. The deepwater harbor attracted steamboats early on, and later, big ships.

While the mills and the railroad had their share of tragedy, the shipwrecks have left the most ghosts in this area.

The worst shipwreck on Puget Sound happened on November 18, 1906. That day, the *Dix*, a 102-foot, 130-ton vessel was headed from the Seattle dock to Bainbridge Island. Seventy-seven people were onboard. Captain Percy Lermond was collecting fares and no one was watching for obstacles. The first officer, who was in charge, steered the steamer directly into a bigger boat.

The *Dix* split in two and sank. In only five minutes, it was gone, killing forty-five of the seventy-seven onboard. The wreckage is still six hundred feet underwater in Puget Sound. Many bodies and parts of the ship were never recovered. If ghosts stay where the people died, imagine all those lost souls under the water!

After another incident, when the *Andelana*—a 304-foot, four-masted British barque, or large sailing ship, sank, stories of curses spread like fire. The year was 1899, and it remains the worst disaster in Tacoma's history.

The crew thought the ship wasn't stable because of the incredibly tall masts. Nine crew members got off in Tacoma, but the captain wouldn't allow the remaining seventeen to leave. He made fun of the ones who were too scared to travel and bullied them. But twenty-four hours later, the last seventeen died, trapped in their sleeping quarters when the ship sank.

The *Andelana* was too top-heavy. It also had no ballast to stabilize it. Plus, a terrible storm raced across the bay with forty-mile-per-hour gusts. All these things combined to create the tragedy.

And after the horrible sinking, came the deadly curses.

A diver tried to reach the *Andelana* in 1935. The leather seal attaching his suit to oxygen ruptured. The man died—and was now the eighteenth death related to the *Andelana*.

Those who died on the boat often reach out, calling to the living. There was a note in a bottle that washed to shore in Mexico two days after the boat sank. Was it sent before the crash or after? Was this a message from the dead?

Visitors to the Port of Tacoma say they've seen a ghostly rowboat disappear on the water. The boat, and sometimes, ghostly swimmers, vanish into the fog around where the *Andelana* sank. There are often cries for help that drift across the water. And some even say they have seen the *Andelana* out at sea, drifting aimlessly.

Ships and boats aren't the only vehicles in Tacoma that have met disaster. In 1900, there was a major streetcar crash. At eight o'clock in the morning, Streetcar Number 116 was headed downtown. It was the Fourth of July, and the roads were packed with people.

The streetcar was meant to carry fifty-five passengers, but about 150 people were crowded onboard. The car hit a sharp curve and couldn't stop. The tracks were wet. The car was going way too fast at fifty miles per hour instead of the usual ten. Some passengers managed to jump off, but for those who stayed, the crash was horrific. Forty-four people died, and over seventy were injured. By 1938, Tacoma had replaced its streetcars with buses and other means of transportation, but still, disaster sites such as this are often haunted by those who died. If you're along the streetcar route, watch out for spirits carrying flags, heading to the ghostly parade.

The Pantages Theater in Tacoma's historic Theater District has hosted ghosts since 1918. A woman named Kate Klondike built the theater to prove to her boyfriend, Alexander Pantages, how much she adored him. But he wasn't impressed. Alexander left her for another woman. Kate remained incredibly sad until the day she died. And now her ghost is said to linger in the theater she built.

Visitors and employees report seeing a woman on the balcony. Is this really Kate? Or

someone else? Whoever it is wears elegant Vaudeville-era clothing, sings ballads in Italian, and makes eye contact with the living before dissipating. There's also a ghost in an usher's uniform who escorts guests to their seats by placing his cold, lifeless hand on their shoulder.

After you visit the theater, check out Point Defiance Park just outside of Tacoma, where there are ten miles of trails, a zoo, an aquarium, and a historic fort. Here, you'll find the spirit of Jennifer Marie Bastian, a young girl who disappeared in the park in August 1986. Her body was found, but the murder remains a mystery. Several people report having seen a ghost girl riding her bike. She vanishes when they get close to her. One witness said they saw a girl smiling at them—but when they checked closer, she had no eyes.

The pagoda at the park is also a spot for paranormal activity: people have reported seeing shadows, hearing disembodied footsteps, and feeling cold drafts.

The mouth of the Puyallup River is another place to find a ghost. The spirit of a man in torn clothes looks angrily at those who come upon him. He catches the eye of people on the street, but then suddenly disappears. It's thought that in the late 1920s and 1930s, during the Great Depression, this area was a campsite for people who'd lost their homes. Perhaps the ghost is still hoping to find someone who will lend him a hand?

Tacoma's Stadium High School was featured in the 1990s movie *10 Things I Hate About You*. The school was originally built in the late 1800s. At the time, it was supposed to be a hotel, but money ran out and that project was abandoned. The unfinished building became a warehouse. A few years later, a fire destroyed much of the building. When it was repaired, it was nicknamed Brown's Castle.

Brown's Castle overlooked a housing area for widows who had lost their husbands at sea. It's said that many of the widows lived the rest of their lives in this spot, waiting for their men to return—but sometimes, their sadness took over and they jumped to their death. One of these ghosts remains.

Teachers and students at the high school have reported a woman in black who lingers, looking out over the ravine. After only a few seconds, the woman's ghost leaps off the cliff and disappears. Over and over, she repeats her jump. The sadness she feels never leaves. If you see her, please, be kind.

Tacoma's Old City Hall, built in 1893, served as the city's government headquarters for fifty years and is reported to be one of the most haunted sites in Washington. The building has been largely vacant since the 1950s. A trickster ghost named Gus is known to haunt the place, stopping the elevators between floors, turning lights on and off, setting off alarms, and throwing objects. Whenever police are called to look for an intruder, they can't find anyone.

Some say Gus might be the ghost of a prisoner held in the building's jail years ago. He might also be the trickster behind many strange occurrences at the Old City Hall. Occasionally, the clock tower bell rings late at night or early in the morning. Security guards have seen floating, shadowy apparitions outside the old council chambers. And there's also a ghost that coughs. (Can ghosts catch colds?)

The Tacoma Hotel once stood near the Pantages Theater. The hotel was built in 1884 to serve Tacoma's best-known and richest visitors. It burned down in 1935, but before that, President Theodore Roosevelt, baseball player Babe Ruth, and author Mark Twain were some of the hotel's most famous guests.

Oddly, the hotel also had a bear. Jack was an eight-hundred-pound brown bear who was like a pet. Jack's mother had been killed by hunters, and they took him home. The hunters eventually sold Jack to the Tacoma Hotel, where he lived in the Bear Garden. His handlers gave him a bath every morning, then served him a cocktail along with his breakfast. In the afternoon, Jack would sit at the bar, just like any other guest, and drink a beer. Everyone was amazed.

Once in a while, Jack would escape at night and walk the streets of Tacoma! One night, when he'd managed to get out of the hotel, a policeman, thinking Jack was dangerous, shot him twice in the side. Sadly, Jack died of his wounds. His body was given to the Washington State History Museum, but in 1958, it was moved out of the display. No one knows where he is now. His spirit, however, is still seen wandering around Tacoma, enjoying his freedom on a late-night walk.

It's said there are ghosts at the University of Puget Sound, and that some of them might be connected to the infamous serial killer, Ted Bundy, who attended the law school there for one year. It's widely thought that Bundy murdered eight-year-old Ann Marie Burr and hid her body in Schiff Hall's cement foundation as it was being built. Students report that her spirit spooks them in dark corners. They hear shuffling feet and have seen a trail of wet slipper marks on the floor.

Bundy confessed to killing thirty-six people, but there could be even more victims. Perhaps some of them are still lingering around the campus at the university? There are stories about bodies hidden in the dorm walls, in abandoned elevator shafts, under basements, and under the floors of dorm rooms. Students also report hearing sounds of wailing and crying coming from empty rooms.

It seems Tacoma has earned the name "Pretty Grit City" for good reason. It's definitely gritty, very pretty, and horribly haunted.

Terrible Travels Outside Tacoma

Algona is a small city in King County, about fifteen miles northeast of Tacoma. In 2020, there were about 3,290 people living there. Looking back, the city was established in the 1870s, though it didn't become officially incorporated until August 22, 1955. Historic cities have many ghosts.

Legend has it that a witch lived in the Old Hotel. Because she was a witch, she could not cast a shadow, so don't look for one. Instead, beware of black cats, listen for disembodied voices and sounds, and be on the lookout for electrical disturbances. You might see spooky things around the building. Is this all from the witch? Or maybe she has friends who've come to visit?

Twenty-eight miles southeast of Tacoma is the Melmont Ghost Town in Carbonado. The town, founded in the early twentieth century, was known for coal mining. There was a train depot, saloon, butcher shop, hotel, store, and housing for the railroad workers.

The town's population slowly dwindled, and in the 1920s, it burned down. Ruins of the former town are still visible, making it easy to imagine what the town looked like one hundred years ago. If you stay a while, you might even meet some of those former residents. Melmont has been described as spooky, and visitors have seen strange movements and heard disembodied voices.

About twenty miles west of Carbonado is the town of Graham. It's located in a rural area with grand views of nearby Mount Rainier. A family who lived in town said they were forced to move away by an angry spirit. Apparently, the ghost of an elderly woman stayed in the home after her husband died of a heart attack in 1994. A psychic told the family that the old woman doesn't realize she's dead. In another house nearby, a man says a ghost is trying to force him to leave, too. What do you think? With so much paranormal activity in this part of Washington, it's quite possible all the homes in Graham will be occupied by ghosts, and the living will have all ... disappeared.

Olalla is twenty-five miles northwest of Tacoma. There, Dr. Linda Burfield and her husband, Sam Hazzard, ran the Starvation Heights Sanitarium. (A sanitarium is a hospital for patients recovering from illness.) They believed they could treat illnesses with extreme starvation because fasting was a form of therapy. Some say more than a dozen people died there. In time, Linda was convicted of forging patients' wills and stealing their valuables. She went to prison.

All that remains of the building is the foundation and incinerator where patients who died at the sanitarium were cremated. With all that happened there, many ghosts have remained behind. Former patients haunt the grounds, including two young boys named Jeff and Kyle. How do we know their names? They've told people, of course. Perhaps they will talk to you, if you decide to visit.

Thornewood Castle, a gothic-tudor style castle, stands in Lakewood, ten miles southwest of Tacoma. It was built in 1911 by Chester Thorne, a business magnate and a founder of the Port of Tacoma. Thorne was also behind the National Bank of Tacoma and Mount Rainier Park. Built by Chester as a gift to his bride, Anna,

Thornewood Castle was nicknamed "the house that love built."

Thorne bought a four-hundred-year-old manor in England and had it taken apart brick by brick. He then shipped the bricks to the United States aboard three ships and rebuilt the manor exactly the same. Now, the castle serves as an inn. There are fifty-four rooms, including twenty-two bedrooms and bathrooms.

Rare hand-painted, stained-glass artwork is mounted in windows throughout the estate, and there are beautiful fountains and gardens outdoors. Guests come for masquerade balls, Shakespearean plays, and film screenings. The castle is listed on the National Register of Historic Places.

And yet, both guests and employees have reported ghosts at Thornewood Castle. One is said to be Chester Thorne himself. He turns on the lights in his former bedroom, which is where he died. He has also been seen on the lawn and near the fountains. Sometimes, he is riding his horse. Other times, he's standing in horseback-riding gear, holding a whip. Witnesses also report seeing the spirit of Thorne's wife, Anna, sitting in the window seat of her room looking out at the garden. Anna's room, now the bridal suite, contains her former mirror. Brides have seen her reflection looking out at them. Spooky!

Employees and guests have reported seeing Chester and Anna together, holding hands at the top of the staircase. They are always dressed for an event, but they don't move. Two of the Thornes' three children have also been reported in the castle. Their eldest daughter sits on the porch, and their son stands on the lawn. Once, there was a ghostly cocktail party, with one hundred ghostly guests dancing, socializing, and drinking. The castle ghosts often play tricks on staff and guests by unscrewing lightbulbs and blowing out candles.

A visit to the area wouldn't be complete without seeing the Meeker Mansion, a grand seventeen-room Victorian mansion in Puyallup. The mansion was built in 1890 by pioneers Eliza Jane and Ezra Morgan Meeker. As a young man, Ezra traveled the Oregon Trail from Iowa to the Pacific Northwest by ox-drawn wagon. Once settled, he grew hops for brewing beer, eventually becoming known as the Hop King of the World. Meeker also served as the first mayor of Puyallup, from 1889 to 1891.

The Meeker Mansion is said to be haunted by the spirits of both Ezra and Eliza Meeker. They are often resting in their old bedroom. Visitors say they've heard Ezra's ghost snoring, while others say they found him in the yard sawing logs. Some claim to have smelled Eliza Meeker's ghostly perfume.

The mansion has been restored and is operated by the Puyallup Historical Society, and it seems that Eliza and Ezra are very happy there.

Cadillac Hotel

Super-scares in Seattle

Coastal Salish Indigenous peoples, including the Duwamish, inhabited the Seattle area long before settlers came in 1851. They'd been there at least four thousand years and created seventeen villages around Elliott Bay. Seattle was named for Duwamish and Suquamish leader Chief Seattle (1786–1866), who helped the settlers. This is Washington's (and the Pacific

Northwest's) largest city. Over 4 million people now live in the area.

In early days, Seattle produced lumber that was shipped to San Francisco and towns in the Puget Sound area. In the 1870s, after coal was discovered near Lake Washington, the Northern Pacific Railway Company came through. The area boomed with logging, coal, fishing, trade, and shipbuilding. Today, Seattle is headquarters for major corporations, including Amazon, Costco, Microsoft, and Starbucks.

With a history like that, it's no wonder old ghosts mingle with more recent deceased spirits.

One of the biggest tragedies happened on June 6, 1889, when The Great Seattle Fire took out all of downtown. Glue boiled over and ignited wood chips in a carpentry shop near Clairmont and Company's cabinet shop. It spread quickly through the sidewalks, streets, and buildings that were all made of wood. The fire department wasn't organized like today, and they lacked the equipment to deal with such a ferocious blaze. The good news was that the fire claimed no human lives. (However, it's believed that one million rats died in the fire. Who wants to meet *those* ghosts? Eww.)

The bad news was that dozens of workers died in the clean up after the fire. The ghosts of these workers are said to haunt the former business district, with sightings of full-body apparitions, orbs, mist or ectoplasm, and cold spots.

Historically, downtown Seattle was originally built at sea level. Because it was low, the city suffered from flooding and sewage problems. The ebb and flow of the tides, and the lack of city planning and proper pipes meant that it smelled terrible and led to illnesses spreading.

After the Great Fire of 1889, the city decided to do something about the problem.

When the city was rebuilt, the street level was raised by about twenty feet. That meant there was now a maze of underground storefronts and tunnels. Today, these tunnels lie below historic Pioneer Square, Seattle's original neighborhood.

In 2020, the Travel Channel program *Portals to Hell* investigated the tunnels, many which are thought to be haunted. Unseen hands shoved the visitors, and ghostly orbs appeared in the dark. Disembodied voices and footsteps were heard echoing through the tunnels.

It's clear to anyone who visits that the undead linger in these musty, dark locations. If you're brave enough, you can take a ghost tour through the tunnels under Seattle. Good luck!

The Klondike Gold Rush in 1897 brought a lot of people to Seattle. Nearly seventy thousand miners flocked to Seattle, hoping to strike it rich. Gold mining was a dangerous job, and a lot of miners died. Some met their end from bad weather or dangerous wildlife. Others died of illness. And a few were killed by their fellow miners in fights.

The ghosts of the miners linger in the hotels where they slept. There are many reports of hauntings. Full body apparitions float down hallways. Disembodied voices and footsteps are often heard. There are orbs, mist, cold spots, and strange temperature changes that can't be explained. Items move on their own. Doors and windows often open and shut on their own.

There are so many ghosts in Seattle, it's amazing there's room for the living, too!

The Hotel Ändra was built in 1926 and originally called the Claremont Hotel. Here, guests have reported hearing glass smashing. On the ninth floor, some say they've heard jazz music and disembodied voices. And some claim to have seen a spirit there as well: a woman wearing 1930s clothing stands in one of the rooms but disappears when guests awaken. It's said this is the spirit of a woman who fell out of a window and died. Now, she haunts the guests. If seeing her isn't scary enough—items are also known to levitate and vanish!

Visit the ghost at the Gessner Mansion (or Georgetown Castle). When you first see it, the mansion is a beautiful and grand building. Wealthy blackjack dealer Peter Gessner built it in 1902. When he died a year later, his spirit remained. Visitors say they've witnessed him with a young woman. Her story is unknown. There's also a ghost baby whose cries can be heard at night. No one is certain who these other spirits belong to, but many have heard or seen them.

A Victorian-style mansion on South Jackson Street was built in 1889. It had a few names through the years, until 1906, when it became the Cadillac Hotel. The place is so crowded with ghosts, you have a good chance to meet one—or two! Here, you can find the ghosts of loggers, fishermen, and railroad and shipyard workers.

The best-known spirits are those of a woman and her child. They've been heard crying at night. It's said the woman was a single mother who had lost her home and took a room at the hotel. Wrapped in sorrow that she couldn't escape, she killed her child and then took her own life. In 2005, the building became part of the National Park Service's Klondike Gold Rush Historical Park, where employees may encounter the ghostly woman and her child while they work.

In 1890, the Merchant's Cafe and Saloon was built. The building, designed by W.E. Boone, a descendant of frontiersman Daniel Boone, is said to be home for several ghosts. A woman's spirit has been seen and heard slamming doors and moving things around. She also turns the bathroom faucets off and on and whispers in men's ears.

A little girl and boy are said to haunt the basement. As the story goes, these children died there in a fire in 1938. Employees report seeing small, shadowy figures. The staff claim that the ghostly children often play tricks on them.

The Harvard Exit Theater was built in 1925 and later became a movie theater in 1968. It is said to be haunted by the spirit of a woman who died in the upstairs lounge. Witnesses say the ghost wears clothing from the 1920s. Terrified employees don't like going upstairs, but they don't like going downstairs, either, because a ghost haunts the first floor. Witnesses say half of his body is solid and the other half is clear or translucent. This downstairs ghost is known as Peter. He wears old-fashioned clothing and likes to play tricks. Finally, another female apparition floats around the building. She's from the Victorian-era and stands as if excited to greet a guest, but if someone reaches out to her, she disappears.

The University Heights School, an elementary school, was built in 1902. It is said to be one of the most haunted buildings in Seattle. A story says that a teacher locked a student named Brian in a closet and forgot about him. This happened on a Friday, and she went home for the weekend, forgetting to unlock the closet door. On Monday, she came back to discover the boy had died.

In another unbelievable story, a ghost boy sits at a classroom desk. Everyone thinks this is Brian. He's been seen walking through the school's halls at night and hiding in the bathroom. Witnesses say Brian's spirit gives off an eerie aura, and if they step into the closet where he was trapped, they feel anger and sadness. There are other phantoms at the school, but unlike Brian, those children play and seem happy.

The Canterbury Ale House hosts the spirit of a man. Legend says that in 1978, a man was shot in the face during a bar brawl and died by the fireplace. Witnesses say they've seen the man's ghost in the mirror. His face is damaged. He turns on the jukebox and plays pranks, scaring employees. Others have reported seeing a dark figure wandering near the bar. Is this the same man? No one knows. He always disappears when approached. There's also a scary symbol, representing death, drawn on the basement floor. No matter how hard anyone tries, it can't be removed.

Martha Washington Park sits along the shore of Lake Washington to the southeast of Seattle. The park is on the site of the former Martha Washington School. The school was demolished in 1989, but the ghosts of those who attended the school still linger.

It's said that long before the school was built, the area was a sacred burial ground for Native Americans. Ghosts have made their presence known through disembodied sobbing and footsteps, floating orbs, showing up in photographs, placing hands on visitors' shoulders, and even *pushing* visitors. A young ghostly girl, wearing a nightgown, scares anyone who sees her.

The Moore Theater is Seattle's oldest entertainment and performing arts venue. The glorious theater was designed by E.W. Houghton and built in 1907. It's decorated with marble and Mexican onyx, solid brass fixtures, and Greek statues. When the theater opened, the Moore could hold 2,500 people and was the third-largest theater in the United States. While official reports say that Kurt Cobain (of the rock group Nirvana) died at home, local legends say it happened at the theater.

The grand and luxurious nine-story Arctic Club was built in 1916, and thousands of Klondike gold miners were members. In 1978, the building was placed on the National Register of Historic Places, and then, it was converted to a DoubleTree hotel. The original building was decorated with stuffed teddy bears and terra cotta walruses. The place was huge. There was a cigar shop, library, barbershop, tearoom, even a bowling alley. Today, though the hotel has been renovated, ghosts are said to haunt the third and fourth floors where visitors often report a phantom whistling sound.

If you're staying in the hotel—listen closely. You might hear whispers about the gold rush, land deals, or perhaps the sound of footsteps. Some say they smell cigar smoke even though the cigar shop closed a long time ago and there's no smoking in the building. There are also ghostly orbs floating in the halls and rooms. Those cool drafts that guests feel, well, they might actually be the spirit of a local politician who died at the hotel.

But most of all, beware of the fifth floor!

After all, that's the floor where Washington's first elected Democratic congressman jumped out a window. Even now, the elevator often stops at the fifth floor, despite no one pressing the buttons.

Visiting Seattle is terrific. See the Space Needle, take a lot of photos, visit the Pike Place Market, and explore the Discovery Park Loop trail. And, of course, don't forget to greet the local ghosts!

More Ghosts Gather Near Seattle

Bainbridge Island (a lovely, small city on an island in Puget Sound) is a thirty-five-minute ferry ride from Seattle. Here, The Madison Diner is said to be haunted by a playful spirit named Harry (possibly the original owner). He makes his presence known by moving items and making disembodied noises.

After breakfast, you can take a series of ferries over to Bremerton, home to several U.S.

Navy facilities, including the Puget Sound Naval Shipyard and the Bremerton Annex of Naval Base Kitsap.

Bremerton Theater (also called the Bremerton Community Theatre) is known to be extremely haunted. Here, you might experience unexplainable noises, floating orbs, movement when no one else is present, doors opening and closing on their own, lights turning on and off on their own, and strange electrical disturbances. Ghost hunters have also captured ghostly responses to questions on their equipment.

One of the most haunted spots in the theater is said to be the costume loft where a ghost nicknamed Captain John is attached to an old military uniform. He gets upset if items are moved. One staff member reported that after she brought a black costume hat home to repair, the pictures on her walls fell off. Frightened, she immediately returned the hat to the theater.

Another staff member reported seeing a pair of green mechanic's pants walking on their own across the stage. If that wasn't scary enough, they also saw strange gray masses sitting on a table that seemed to be talking to each other. They disappeared as quickly as they had appeared.

Others have reported a full-body ghostlike image and the shadow of a man in a top hat and cape. Is he there to scare or greet? Perhaps he's simply enjoying the show.

The Frank Chopp Apartments were first used as the City General Hospital. The hospital opened in 1918 to deal with the Spanish flu pandemic. In 1942, the building became the Harrison Memorial Hospital, and later, it served as a nursing home. It's not known how many patients and residents passed away there, but it appears that they still consider the place home. The living report hearing disembodied voices and footsteps. Ghostly children play in the halls.

Lights turn on and off on their own. And there is a ghostly nurse who walks through walls, still caring for her ghostly patients.

Bremerton's Holland Road is so haunted that it's often called Ghost Road. It's said that an elderly man was hit by a car late at night while he was gathering mail from his mailbox. Farther down, a young girl was tragically killed while riding her horse. Along the road, people have reported seeing strange, shadowy shapes. Some claim that they've seen the girl, who had long black hair, riding her horse. Some drivers come at night, hoping to catch the strange shadows and spirits, which are said to appear more often in thick fog.

The USS *Turner Joy* (DD-951), a destroyer, is docked in Bremerton, (a destroyer is a fast warship that escorts larger ships in a fleet.) The ship was used during the

Vietnam War and now serves as a museum. Some visitors and staff have seen three ghostly sailors who remain on board. Other visitors have felt a strange presence watching them as they tour the ship. Cold spots have been reported. During one ghost investigation, an investigator sensed an invisible presence following her. Fully charged camera batteries were suddenly drained with no explanation. Was a ghost trying to make them stop filming? Or using the battery energy to power himself?

Des Moines, Washington, is about sixteen miles south of Seattle. Founded in 1889, it is named for Des Moines, Iowa, because several early settlers came from there. The ghost of a little girl named Diana walks the Des Moines Beach Park each year on January 8. During an investigation, ghost hunters reported that their cameras suddenly turned off. A psychic in the group reported seeing a ghostly young girl walking up a trail with a group of children's spirits. The girl warned the investigators to stay away from the "crabby old man." It's not clear why Diana and the other children haunt the area, but something traumatic must have happened to them there.

Edmonds in Snohomish County, about seventeen miles north of Seattle, was established in 1876 by loggers. Built in 1906, the majestic Edmonds Opera House has ghosts in the attic, basement, and other spots in the building. Ghost hunters say their electronic devices light up right away after entering, detecting paranormal electrical impulses. Orbs have been seen, and costumes tossed around. And a woman visitor claims to have been pushed down the stairs by an unseen force.

Kent, in King County, is about twenty miles south of Seattle. The historic old train station in the city, built in 1927, is home to a ghost train. People report seeing the train heading straight at them at random times of night, only to vanish and reappear on the other side of the crossing. Also, the Bereiter House, now home to the Greater Kent Historical Society and Kent Museum, is said to be haunted. Staff and visitors have reported objects being moved by an invisible force. There are cold spots, disembodied ghostly voices, and the unexplained sounds of bells ringing.

Port Orchard, across Puget Sound from Seattle, was originally settled in 1854. Over 160 years later, in 2015, a photographer decided to drive into a nearby forest to take photos of the sunset. He parked his car so that he could make some adjustments on his camera. When he put his vehicle in reverse, he looked into his rear-view mirror—there was a young girl with dark brown hair and marble-like eyes sitting in the back seat, staring expressionlessly back at him. The man stared at the young girl for a few seconds, petrified to turn around and look behind him. He was so scared that he turned off the car, yanked the keys out of the ignition, and jumped out of the vehicle. When he gathered his courage and peered into the car again—the girl was gone.

Before we leave the Seattle area, you should know that Indigenous peoples have lived in the Puget Sound region for at least ten thousand years. They are known as Coastal Salish, with tribes including Duwamish, Nisqually, Skagit and Snoqualmie. Today, there are nine Indigenous reservations in the Puget Sound region, including the Squaxin, Nisqually, Puyallup, Muckleshoot, Suquamish, Stillaguamish, Tulalip, Swinomish and Upper Skagit. There are three additional tribes that are recognized by the U.S. government but do not have reservations: the Snoqualmie, Samish and Skykomish. Finally, the Duwamish and Steilacoom are working for federal recognition. Collectively, these tribes are referred to as the Lushootseed peoples.

One legend has it that Seattle's Pike Place Market is built on top of an Indigenous burial ground. It's said the daughter of Chief Seattle (for whom Seattle is named), Princess Angeline—or, in her tribal language, Kikisoblue—wanders there among the shops and restaurants. If you see her, she's small and wears a red head covering. Her ghostly mission is to protect ancestral lands.

Next time you visit Pike Place Market, watch for her.

And ask her to tell you her story...

Eerie Everett

Located twenty-five miles north of Seattle and with over 110,000 residents, Everett is the seventh-largest city in Washington.

The area was originally home to the Snohomish people, and the city was incorporated in 1893 after the Great Northern Railway arrived. Industry came, and several sawmills were built. In 1967, Boeing, a large aircraft manufacturer, built an assembly plant at Paine Field. Boeing remains the city's largest employer.

When a fire destroyed the YMCA in the 1920s, the building's janitor, George, helped several children escape the fire, but he tragically died in the flames and smoke. Witnesses still hear George's voice over the intercom. He also moves exercise equipment around the gym. George obviously still takes his job very seriously.

Everett High School's auditorium is haunted by a maintenance worker who was killed in a renovation project. Both teachers and students have reported seeing the man's ghostly image. Some call him the "Blue Ghost." Although he hangs around all the time, he never helps with homework.

The Historic Everett Theatre opened in November 1901. There are several ghosts reportedly haunting the theater. One is a male with a big, bushy mustache. Staff call him Smiling Al because he's always grinning. When

Al is around, doors open and close on their own, and lights turn themselves on and off. In 1993, workers on the building reported feeling watched. One staff member said he was leaving a room and couldn't close the door. The harder he tried, the more resistance he felt. Suddenly, the door flew open! The force knocked the worker to the floor. Another employee once saw a sweater lift off the floor in the projection room, float in midair, then fall to the floor. A third employee felt like he was being watched. When he looked up from the film projector, he saw the top half of a man looking at him through the window. A moment later, the ghostly being disappeared.

Everett is extra eerie!

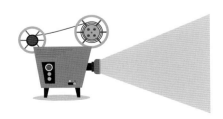

Small Towns with Spooky Spirits

Port Gamble is northwest of Seattle on the shores of the scenic Hood Canal. Although the town has fewer than one thousand residents, it had one of the world's largest continuously operating sawmills from 1853 to 1995. Some of the buildings are preserved, making it a place frozen in time.

The Victorian Walker-Ames House was built in 1889 by William Walker, the sawmill's master mechanic. Haunted tours are popular in the house, because long after their deaths, William and his family, plus a few of their friends, are still there. Visitors report ghostly images, disembodied voices, footsteps on the second floor, wet footprints in hallways, impressions left on an old chair, cold spots and unexplained temperature changes, windows opening and closing on their own, female visitors having their hair pulled, jackets being tugged, odd smells, and ghostly images in photographs. That's a *lot* of spooky stuff! And that's not all—there are said to be young spirits at play, including a young girl named "Annabelle."

The theater in Port Gamble is also known for its paranormal activity. One story about the

theater is that during an intermission, a woman, tired of waiting in the long ladies' room line yelled into the men's room: "Is there anyone in here?" A voice responded, "No, it's all free, come on in." She did. But there was no one in there!

Whidbey Island, at the northern edge of Puget Sound, is the fourth-largest island in the contiguous forty-eight states. The population of Coupeville, on Whidbey Island, is around two thousand but doesn't include all the ghosts. The Captain Whidbey Inn dates to the early twentieth century. A "gray lady" is rumored to haunt the hotel. She's not alone. Young girls can be heard giggling, and in another room, there is a bed that always looks like someone has been laying on top of the covers.

Fort Casey is situated in the middle of the island. This U.S. military base was constructed in 1897. Today, it's a state park with camping, boating, hiking, historic officer's quarters—and creepy underground passageways. Unexplained events at the fort include scratching sounds, apparitions that appear and disappear quickly, and a disembodied woman's voice and screaming.

The former navy exchange on Whidbey Island, built in 1942, is said to be haunted. (A navy exchange is a store for members of the U.S. Navy.) There are stories of a spirit nicknamed "the Lurker" who drops pennies and leaves popcorn, making a huge mess. Strangely, there is no popcorn machine at the exchange. So, where did it come from?

The Colonel Walter Crockett House, built in the 1850s, is rumored to be haunted. Now a bed-and-breakfast, guests report hearing moaning and something like smashing glass. A hand-shaped bloodstain has been observed on the ceiling, scaring even the bravest visitors.

Ghosts of children have been seen in the old one-room San de Fuca schoolhouse. A woman who took a nap on the lawn there said a group of mischievous, ghostly kids shouted at her to "Wake up!" They quickly disappeared. She didn't stick around to see if they would reappear.

The San de Fuca schoolhouse was for sale in 2023. The house has views of Penn Cove and the surrounding mountains. It was built in 1902 but has had a lot of changes, like a new great room and updated kitchen. It's not cheap to buy

a haunted house. This one sold for $600,000. Would you want to live there?

The Moran Mansion at the Rosario Resort was built by millionaire Robert Moran. It has five floors and eighty-eight rooms. The resort is said to be haunted by Alice Goodfellow Rheem, nicknamed the Lady in Red. Alice was the wife of the resort's second owner, Donald Rheem. The hotel is now a museum. Alice's ghost seems to prefer roaming around the second and third floors. Some say she's mischievous, playing tricks or clip-clopping down the hallways in heeled shoes.

The Hotel de Haro in San Juan Island's Roche Harbor Resort in Friday Harbor was built in 1886. The ghost of Adah Beeny, a governess and secretary for a family who ran businesses on the island, is still opening doors, turning on appliances, and moving items around. One woman reported her hands went numb as she entered the hotel's lobby because the hotel was "so haunted."

These islands may be small, but if you visit, you will probably run into a ghost or two!

Herald Building

Who's Haunting Bellingham?

Bellingham is situated eighteen miles south of the Canadian border along Bellingham Bay on the northern edge of Puget Sound.

There, the Bayview Cemetery is a public park that was founded in 1887. Locals say you should never walk around the cemetery at night because of the ghosts that flit among the tombstones and make strange noises. One monument in the cemetery is even nicknamed the Death Bed.

Legend says that any living person who lies on it will speed up their own death. Another monument is called Angel Eyes, and the spirit of the body buried there is said to roam the cemetery.

The Bellingham Herald Building is home to the city's newspaper. Built in 1926, the building's elevator moves from floor to floor on its own, as if carrying a ghostly passenger. It might be because a former elevator operator was murdered in the building, and he is still hard at work, doing his job.

Mount Baker Theatre opened in 1927. While searching for ghosts in the theater, investigators recorded disembodied voices and reported full-body ghostly images, cold spots, and balls of light. They determined that more than four different ghosts haunt the theater. One is a young woman named Judy, who calls out the names of employees across the stage. The others are unknown but visitors say they've been touched on their backs and shoulders by unseen hands.

The Old Town Café staff report hearing disembodied piano music in the restaurant. They've seen dishes and other kitchen items floating on their own. A female ghost in a white old-fashioned dress has been spotted on the second floor.

If you're visiting Bellingham, beware!

The Final Frights

The last two stops on our ghostly tour of Puget Sound are the coastal cities of Port Townsend and Port Angeles.

Port Townsend on Washington's Quimper Peninsula was Washington's first major port and a boomtown in the 1850s. Though the town attracted a tough crowd, it was also called the City of Dreams.

The Ann Starrett Mansion was built in 1889.

It now serves as a bed-and-breakfast, and it's apparently so cozy that several ghosts like to stay here, too! One is described as a red-haired woman in a white gown. She's been spotted floating throughout the building and on the main stairs. This might be Ann Starrett herself. Her husband George has been seen there, too, as has the family's nanny, who can be recognized by her black dress.

The Holly Hill House was built in 1872. A man in old-fashioned clothing haunts a bedroom on the top floor. The room smells like cigar smoke, which might be because William Hill died in the home's parlor and still haunts the house.

The impressive Manresa Castle was built in 1892. At the time, it was the city's largest private residence, with thirty rooms. It's now a hotel. Two known ghosts remain there: a young woman named Kate who leaped out of the window in room 306, and a monk who, legend has it, died in the tower above room 302. Guests can stay in these two rooms, if they're feeling brave enough for one overnight. Do you have the courage?

The beautiful Palace Hotel, built in 1889, is believed to be haunted by as many as ten ghosts. There's the ghost of a lady in an old-fashioned blue dress nicknamed the "Lady in Blue," who has been seen in rooms 3 and 4. Her spirit brings the strong scent of perfume. Captain Tibbals, the hotel's builder and former owner, has also been reported in the building. An old woman in a black dress stands near the stove in room 3's kitchen. There's a friendly little boy named Adam who has been seen running and playing on the third floor. A menacing, shadowy apparition occasionally follows guests down the third-floor hallway. The ghosts of a woman and her children are said to haunt several floors. If you stay at the hotel, there's a book where guests can record their paranormal experiences. Be sure to take a close look as you turn the book's pages . . . some of the entries may just be out of this world!

At the Monarch Hotel, formerly the Water Street Hotel, you can find male apparitions in old-fashioned top hats walking the halls at night. Built in 1889 for only $25,000 by a pharmacist, the hotel is a beautiful, three-story Victorian building with waterfront views. Ghostly orbs have been photographed and videotaped. Strange noises fill the lobby at night. Three deaths are said to have taken place there, and at least one of the dead still wanders around the building, but who is it? No one knows for sure.

Just a few miles away, Port Townsend's Fort Worden opened in 1902. The fort was home to almost one thousand soldiers and officers training to defend Puget Sound from enemy forces. Now, there's a ghostly woman who peeks out the second-floor window of the old hospital every night at around ten-thirty. Visitors have also reported seeing a former guard dressed in an army sergeant's uniform, who seems to be carrying on with his duties.

An hour away, popular Port Angeles is known for fishing, but you need to know the town's origins before you visit. This historic city had so much flooding early on that the entire town was raised in 1914. Now ghost tours are popular because it's said that spirits haunt the tunnels beneath the modern town. Sign up for a haunted tour and maybe you'll see ghostly faces stare out from old windows, or meet ghosts trapped in the underground.

For even *more* scares, drive just eighteen miles to Crescent Lake, home to the legendary Lady of the Lake. In life, the lady was thirty-five-year-old Hallie Illingworth. She was a waitress at the nearby Lake Crescent Lodge, and in 1937, she disappeared. Three years later, her body was found. Her husband, Monty, was convicted of second-degree murder and sentenced to life in prison. When he got out of prison, he moved to California, but Hallie's ghost is still haunting the lake and surrounding area. Her spirit drifts along the lake's shore and over the water, glowing pale and translucent.

While these are the last stops on our ghostly tour, there are more spirits to be discovered around Port Angeles and Port Townsend. Beware of chilly breezes. Keep your eyes open for orbs. And if there's a hand on your shoulder, turn slowly—you never know who, or what, you might find!

A Ghostly Goodbye

From the beginning of time, people have told ghost stories. These stories are often a mix of truth, exaggeration, fear, humor, and wishful thinking. The more interesting tales became legends, passed from one generation to the next.

Come visit Washington. You can hike, bike, boat, camp, fish, shop, sample some delicious food—and look for ghosts! The history of the area includes the many people who came to build their homes there. Ghosts and spirits linger in the parks, cemeteries, hotels, and restaurants.

Ghosts are waiting in Puget Sound—waiting for *you*—if you dare to meet them.

New York Times bestselling author **Stacia Deutsch** has written more than three hundred children's books, including *The Jessie Files*, a spin-off of the beloved *Boxcar Children* mystery series. Stacia lives in Temecula, California, where she is a member of the historical society. She loves hearing spooky stories! Find her online at www.staciadeutsch.com, @staciadeutsch_writes, and www.facebook/staciadeutsch.

Check out some of the other *Spooky America* titles available now!

   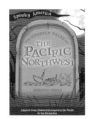

Spooky America was adapted from the creeptastic *Haunted America* series for adults. *Haunted America* explores historical haunts in cities and regions across America. Here's more from the original *Haunted Puget Sound* author, Ira Wesley Kitmacher:

 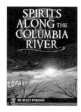 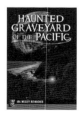